Foodie Dessertations

BITE SIZED RECIPES OF FOODIE-LICIOUS POETRY

by

ROBERT C SAUNDERS

Dynamically Activated, LLC

What people are saying about
Foodie Dessertations:

"The play on words leaves my brain stimulated and strangely desiring more."

Robin Liginos
Food service industry

"These dessertations entangle all of your senses at once."

Joshua Stevens
Mechanical technician

"This made me hungry, it's great writing, loved it! I could read this over and over just in case I missed something. Super intelligent!"

Michael J. Silva
Dunkin Donuts Franchisee St. Petersburg, Florida

"A foodilicious tongue tantalizing romp!"

Johnny Morales
General Manager of Aqua Prime Seafood & Steaks

Book cover design by Bayprint

Photograph provided by Vanessa Protic of Demure-Lynn Photography

Publisher: Dynamically Activated, LLC
304 37th Ave N
Suite 310
St. Petersburg, Fl 33704
dynamicallyactivated@gmail.com

Visit the author website:
www.robertcsaunders.com
www.dynamicallyactivated.com

ISBN: 978-0-9982692-4-5 (eBook)
ISBN: 978-0-9982692-8-3 (Paperback)

POETRY/ GENERAL

Version: 2018.05.16

This book is dedicated

to my niece, Jonetia

and

nephews, James and Jairre

who always appreciated great food and all that accompanied it.

OTHER BOOKS

BY

ROBERT C. SAUNDERS

Nurses Bred for Business:
The Awakening Of Legions Of Nurse Entrepreneurs

Dances in the Theater of the Mind

Rythmic Elegance:
A poetic treatise on our place in the universe

TABLE OF CONTENTS

PREFACE

I want to say up front that I am not on any psychiatric medications, yet, though my wife thinks I need something. It's that whole fine line between genius and insanity phenomenon playing itself out, maybe? Any who, I do believe that food speaks to the very core of what makes us humans. We emotionalize it, humanize it, demonize it, spiritualize it, romanticize it, psychoanalyze it and in so many ways impute to it far more than our ancestors did.

Our forebearers ate to survive only and now at the other end of the spectrum food, for some, is the center of life itself! I am merely advocating a somewhat balanced middle ground where one can derive pleasure, humor, satiety, from finely prepared dishes that elevate the dining experience. Beyond that, a psychiatric consult could be in order.

As you read on you will encounter puns, spoofs, prose and any other literary device I could employ. I am not sure what I had more fun doing, experimenting with and tweaking the recipes or cooking up these poems, you decide. Also, at the back of the book I attempt to thank absolutely everyone that I could think of that I took poetic license with. Thank you all for your support.

I want S'mores out of life

Who does not crave a life of greater caloric meaning?
Deeper soul searching snackishfaction?
To find it ooooooh! What sectioned gleaning!

O that I would weigh it's preciousness graham for crispy graham,
delectableness marshaled in mellowed cocoa jam?!?

Ah, to the ascent of controlled roasting,
can one be faulted for sticky sweet boasting?

One cannot, desireth I, a snack man apart who.....
merely wants S'mores out of life.

S'mores Pizza

1 can refrigerated thin pizza crust dough
½ cup chocolate hazelnut spread
2 whole cinnamon graham crackers, finely crushed
1 cup semi-sweet chocolate morsels
3 cups miniature marshmallows
6 servings

Lettuce pray

Heavenly farmer, help us allay our sandwich fears,
romaine with us through stacked cold cut stares.

Please mayo pack flavor into taste bud signs,
mixed greens to fill us with pulled pork hope designs.

Lettuce be thankful, tomatoes sliced are guaranteed to no man,
and good meals are no accident, they are always planned,
now we must pay as the sandwich delivery guy is double
parked with food in hand.

Chicken Cashew Lettuce Wraps

1 tablespoon rice vinegar

1 tablespoon brown sugar

2 cloves garlic, minced

¼ teaspoon ground red pepper

¼ teaspoon ground ginger

1 teaspoon sesame oil

2 ½ tablespoons soy sauce, divided

3 tablespoons Canola oil or oil of choice

2 pieces chicken breast, total diced approx. ¾ Lb.

1 cup onion, diced

½ head of lettuce

4-6 servings

Kidney bean fame

Notoriously laden in kidney beans,
prominence emerges from Hollywood kitchen scenes.

JFKidney Jr. arises from presidential cold bean salads,
Kidney Perry sings in Indian styled bean chili ballads.

Kidney Rock plays on in Aunt Patsy's famous beef stew flurry,
Nicole Kidney's guest appearance causes quite a stir in a red
beaned hurry, quickly elevated the vegan bean and
mushroom curry.

Kidney Chesney's performance really brought it to
the corn and pomegranate summer suprising,
and who expected Kidney Kardashian and
Quinoa West in 5 bean paparazzi uprising?

Kidney bean soup

1 pound dried kidney beans or 3 (14 ounce) cans
2 onions, chopped
½ teaspoon dried oregano
2 garlic cloves, chopped
1 jalapeno, diced optional
1 14 ounce can tomatoes, chopped
1 tablespoon tomato paste
1 tablespoon cumin
¼ teaspoon cayenne powder
1 tablespoon paprika
6 servings

Missing: one stray martini

Please help me find my lovable dash of vermouth,
O my vodka baby! Likes to have its chilled belly
shaken and at times stirred, kudos to the man
or woman that savors thee.

It gets dirty easily and has a distinct tasteful personality,
often gets lost in cocktail lounges with
a party mood formality.

Answers to many names: OO7,
Money Penny or Diamonds are Forever,
can be lured easily with
tooth picked olives though
it thinks it is quite clever.
If seen call 1800drinkup

Orangatang cocktail

½ oz Malibu coconut rum
½ oz banana liqueur
½ teaspoon grenadine syrup
3 oz half and half
1 ½ oz orange juice
1 serving

Desserted again

Yes! It has happened again, another dinner date, another party,
another late meal of fine dining, how could I be so gullible?
Shame on me, desserted again!! I can't help my whining!
My wife is to blame too, yes, that sweet toothed monster!
That that pompous puppeteer of pastries!
It is true, its sooo.....true!

Stacking my plate high with deliciously
derisive delights and you've seen her, sick grin
painted on her attractive demeanor.
Sultry temptation pours from her lips:
"What do you want for dessert?
There! GUILTY by her own admission!!!
Don't be beguiled by her perfect dentition.

No end to caloric bombshells catapulted at my plate,
I don't know how much more of this I can tolerate,
must find a non desserted exit before it is too late!!!

Oh, curse you Sara Lee and Ghirardelli............desserted again!

Sara Lee Kalhua White Russian Brownies

2 (3 ounces) package cream cheese, softened
3 eggs
1 ½ cup sugar
1 ¼ cup flour
6 tablespoons butter
½ cup unsweetened cocoa
¼ teaspoon baking powder
¼ teaspoon salt
1 cup Kahlua
½ cup Vodka
8 servings

O my garlic dreamer

Yes, so pleasing my garlic dearest,
in too much company I try to get near lest.
The pungency of your majesty, disseminated
best while sleep spared would be a great travesty.

Stimulating my immunity, safe from troubled living,
tickling my tummy, runneth me near thine porcelain throne,
still I love the stews and pot roast you've blessed slumbering,
simmering through to the bone.

Whether roasted, diced or placed whole in my restful steamer,
the savory aromatic effervescence you exude until tomorrow
night, sleep well o my garlic dreamer.

Chicken with roasted garlic pan sauce

One 4 ½ to 5 lb. chicken, rinsed and patted dry
Kosher salt and pepper
1 head of garlic, halved crosswise, plus 2 cloves, minced
1 tablespoon extra virgin olive
½ cup minced yellow onion
½ cup minced green bell pepper
½ cup dry white wine
1 bay leaf
Pinch of dried thyme
4 servings

That's how she works

Taste the coffee of her altruism,
the flavored creamers that is her style,
served with ginger cookies of happy days
that is characterized in her smile.

Cupboards stockpiled, bursting with wifely hospitality,
friendly feelings boxed and thin minted pure without formality.

Loves what she loves in people dipped in chocolate experiential,
the crumpets of inner joy married to flavored teas served
providential.

With the passing of time these strange little quirks,
I appreciate this ethic, the what, the why,
the way how she works.

Caramel coffee

8 teaspoons ground Maxwell House coffee
½ cup caramel ice cream topping
6 cups cold water
½ cup thawed Cool Whip whipped topping
4 teaspoons chocolate covered toffee bar, chopped
6 servings

Garlic floozy

My how easily thee strays, in seasoning ways.

Sprinkled on this tart bread, soaking with that sleazy stew,
rubbing on any rump roast you see, get a hold of yourself!
What is the matter with you?

What's that? You want to flirt with my herb garden?
Your fresh! Once people get a whiff of this broiling
soupy drama of aromatizing ways, it is sure to wreak
havoc in seductively shameless cooking displays.

It will be over between us! So what if I'm choosy,
I only love you Italian bread!! There! I said it
....you garlic floozy.

Herb-Crusted rib roast with mustard cream sauce

1 (7-8 lb.) bone-in easy carve rib roast, trimmed

Salt and pepper

1 cup finely chopped fresh parsley leaves

2 large egg whites, lightly beaten

4 garlic cloves, finely chopped

2 tablespoon minced fresh oregano

2 tablespoon minced fresh rosemary

3 tablespoon olive oil

1 cup dry white wine

1 cup heavy cream

2 tablespoon Dijon mustard

8-10 servings

Gingers grumbling again

Why only a ½ teaspoon of me?,
if this is a food challenge
and you endeavor to win it,
I may not be part of an all female singing group
but don't you know that everything is still better
with a little ginger in it?

Just look back through ancient recipe pages,
of royal world class chefs, Benedictine monks and Hindu sages,
from appetizers to romantic feasts, oh yeah, I'm what all the rage is.

Fantastic to the taste buds lights,
a celebrity among gastronomic delights.
From classy to straight up gangsta smack,
I'm an egotistically spiced bigot so forget
the rest and take me 1st off the rack.

Gingerbread crinkle cookies

1 (14.5-oz) box gingerbread cake mix
1/3 cup vegetable oil
2 large eggs
1 teaspoons pumpkin pie spice
1/3 cup powdered sugar
4 servings

Judged by my pears

I cannot escape pearfect judgement!
Whether I hide by the Bartlett pear tarts,
they mock my fruited kitchen smarts.

Cool it! Back up off of me all of you pear sorbets.
That's right, I'm talking to you, Anjou, Anjou, Anjou!!
I know what all of you are thinking:
"His Asian pear salad has fallen from grace,
no Concorde will be reached by grilled disgrace."
(condescending fruitlike laughter echos)

I don't have to listen to ANY of this!!
Your not the Bosc of me. (stated in icy contemplative repose)
Ah, redemption can be found in French butter pear cakes,
sipped with Comice pear cocktail jubilation! In one more
Seckel, I will no longer be judged by my pears.

French pear tart

1½ cups all-purpose flour
¼ teaspoon salt
5 tablespoons sugar
12 tablespoons unsalted butter, melted
8 large pears, washed
3 tablespoons unsalted butter
1 tablespoons water
¾ cup fig preserves
8 servings

The Hershey bar

"Oh finally! Hershey is...
Excuse me Swiss Miss, are we familiar? No?!
I thought sure I saw you at the corner of rich and cocao,
enjoying refined brown confection sugared high,
now running low, had too much you know...
(30 servings is my limit, must display self
control in these chocolated matters)

Sure it wasn't you? No way say you?
it was some "other" naughty nibbler,
pandering to sin stenciled mass
produced confectionary blocks,
get behind thee candied quibbler!

It's okay, chocolate addiction is not punishable crime
(sayeth the tempter to the temptee.)
In fact, I will even go with you to the Hershey bar.

Hershey bar pie

1 graham cracker pie crust
1 stick butter
6 almond (Hershey bars)
12 ounces cool whip
8 servings

"Bad Beans: The Musical" Reviews

What people are saying:

"Absolutely mesmerized by the dutch oven special effects!
They really let it rip repeatedly."
Gary Enema of **The Connecticut Constipator**

"This production explodes on the scene in a way most fiberous
choreography just can't deliver."
Bill Bottoms of **The Bloated Challenger**

"These Bad Beans were born to dazzle! This is the musical fruit
your grandchildren won't forget."
Regul R. Flushings of **The Smooth Mover**

"A colonic tour de force."
Bari Atric author of **Gaseous Fixations aren't Bad**

Three-bean barbecue

6 slices Oscar Mayer bacon
1 onion, chopped
16 ounces baked beans
15 ½ ounces butter beans, rinsed
15 ounces kidney beans, rinsed
¾ cup Bull's Eye barbecue sauce
½ teaspoon dry mustard
8 servings

I came face to face with the Devil

First, I saw him in my blueberry
waffles, made them stone cold,
then he possessed my sausage links
despite being biscuit rolled.

The last straw, Satan was in my bacon strips and
I knew not what to do, then I said a fervent prayer and ...
I ATE THE DEVIL THRU AND THRU!!!!

Bacon sausage overnight breakfast casserole

1 pack bacon

12 ounces sausage-either bulked spiced, or links

1 onion

1 bell pepper, any color sliced in strips

2 cloves garlic

5 ounces smoked gouda cheese shredded

5 ounces mozzarella-shredded

8 cups French bread-slightly stale, cut into one inch cubes

2 cups dried tomatoes

2 cups fresh leafy greens, chopped using spring mix

12 eggs

2 cups half & half

¼ cup Dijon mustard

8-12 servings

If Madea was your breakfast partner

Don't think I haven't heard about your
sausage ways girl, mmmmHmmm!

Dipping them in maple syrup sweet,
along with sugary cereal for a real
breakfast treat.

You don't learn, go ahead,
keep rolling up them sausage biscuits.
I hate to have to say this but you're
a sausage gravy misfit!!

See, what you need is breakfast healin!
Yes Lord! Heal this child!! (Looking heavenward)
What's that? You're going to Golden Corral for breakfast?
Ok, ok,.....pick you up at 9.

Biscuits and sausage gravy

2 tablespoons butter
1 recipe buttermilk biscuits
4 breakfast sausage patties
2 tablespoons all-purpose flour
2 cups skim milk
to taste, salt and pepper
6-8 servings

I love that

I love that we get along so well,
Respectful
Kindly
Considerate that's swell

Even at breakfast we can shar...

HANDS OFF MY PANCAKE
STACK BUB!!

MOVE IT OR LOSE IT!!!

(Except for breakfast, our relationship is not dangerous.)

Apple Pancake

3 tablespoons butter
1 large apple, cored and sliced
½ cup white sugar, divided
2 teaspoons ground cinnamon
4 eggs
½ cup milk
½ cup all purpose flour
1 teaspoon baking powder
1 teaspoon vanilla extract
1 pinch salt
2-4 servings

I've seen you with that you know who

Always flirting among the hickory smoked chips,
savory salt and pepper desire dripping from her lips,
With sunny side up eggs hanging from her wavy hips.

I try not to be overly sensitive and at breakfast I'm not fussy,
But I don't like the way you keep smackin down that BACON
HUSSY!!!

Best bacon ever

1 pack bacon, thick sliced
½ cup brown sugar
3 teaspoons chili powder
1-2 servings

http://www.thefoodhussy.com/2017/05/food-hussy-recipe-bacon-horseradish.html

Love takes 3 meals

As a rule:
1. Breakfast is...
      Chocolate!

2. Lunch is...
      Chocolate!

3. Dinner is...
      Chocolate!

{Disclaimer: My wife had input on this one}

5-Minute microwave Fudge

1 (12-oz.) bag semisweet chocolate chips

1 (14-oz) can sweetened condensed milk

¼ cup creamy almond butter

1 ¼ cups roughly chopped honey roasted almonds

½ teaspoon coarse sea salt

12 servings

Foodie rapper Wolfgang Puck

Wolfgang Puck finally found his
rap voice and has a hot new single out.....

Rollin Up My Biscuits!

Lyric sampling:

"Droppin zem hot zso smooth und hand craafted qvuick,
If I'm a kitchen atelete zhen it's about to go down thiick,
Just make szure I'm a food netwurk 1st roound drafft pick!"

Keep elevating your craft bro! pizza out.

Wolfgang's buttermilk biscuits recipe

1-1/2 cups all-purpose (plain) flour
1-1/4 cups cake flour
1-1/2 tablespoons sugar
1 tablespoon plus 1 teaspoon baking powder
2 teaspoons salt
¼ teaspoon baking soda
10 tablespoons (5 ounces) chilled unsalted butter, cut into small pieces
1 cup organic buttermilk
1 to 2 tablespoons milk or cream
Makes 20-22 biscuits
http://ihavenet.com/recipes/wolfgang-puck-recipe-Buttermilk-Biscuits.html

I can't beer your wine-ing

The bickering over Chardonnays',
your bougie Pinot Noir displays.

Bimini Twists and Reef Donkey spats,
Worst yet you're off key baseball stats.

You do realize your draft beer choices are wearing my patience
thin, Oh... you're going bar hopping? Where and when?

Cranberry Pinot Noir meatballs

1 (1 pound 10 ounce) bag Italian style meatballs
1 (16 ounce) can whole cranberry sauce
1 teaspoon brown mustard, spicy
1 cup Robert Mondavi Private Selection Pinot Noir
1 cup brown sugar, packed
20 servings

Wrapped in affection?

We're all still like babies needing:
    -Safety
    -Security
    -Feel loved, at that dearly
    -Emotional connection for surely
    -Physical touch profoundly effective
    -Alter our life experience good or defective
    -We cry out silently still subtle unspoken
      whether from Kathmandu to Hoboken

You want milk, cookies and a nappy now don't you?

Almond butter chocolate chip cookies

1 cup unsalted almond butter, stirred well
¾ cup Sucanat
1 large egg
½ teaspoon baking soda
¼ teaspoon sea salt
3 oz dark chocolate (70%-cocoa or greater), broken into small pieces
6-8 servings

Trouble with the No Name dip

I'm having trouble getting rid of this No Name dip,
Loves to hang out with the cool ranch whip,
He's so convinced that he is God's gift yet
no one will let him cross their lips.

Wants to remain the center of taste bud nips,
doesn't go together with jokes or chips,
Despite all this he's clueless, tasteless,
tactless and won't come to grips.

No name chip dip

1 pack cream cheese (must be room temperature or lumps will appear)
3 tablespoons mayo
3 tablespoons chili sauce
2 tablespoons finely chopped onion
20 servings

I saw JFK Jr. in Walmart

All done up in full photographic rigors,
exuding confident utility next to the
Chips Ahoy and Snickers.

Plenty of tabloid bubble gum for light
minded magazine chewing, either leave him
behind or purchase quick for this is the end of
fast lane check out viewing.

No bake Chips Ahoy! Icebox cake

45 Original Chips Ahoy cookies
(Approximately 2 packages, plus 2 extra for garnish)
4 cups heavy cream
3 tablespoons sugar
1 teaspoon vanilla
8-12 servings

Where is my thermometer?

Oh my, come quick, I'm so sick with this,
the sugar flu and cocoa so ubiquitous.

So feverish with sweet cream and almond bliss,
brown confection as consequence my dying wish.

Dr Whitman! Dr Cadbury! please take note,
Wow! I'm so relieved my chocolate fever broke.

Cadbury crack

2 sleeves salted Saltines crackers
1 ½ cups salted butter
½ cup shaved coconut
½ package Cadbury eggs
1 package chocolate chips
1 teaspoon vanilla
1 ½ cups brown sugar
8 servings

Immiment grazer

Nearly had an altercation
as grocery cart brushed
by the Stella Doro bread sticks,
staring provocatively my way on aisle 6.
No! must stay strong as my wife rudely smacks
my hands from nibbling on grocery section
strawberry fresh picks.

Those snickers in the marked down Jumbo pack
are in more trouble than they know,
why women torture their hungry
men is just not appropo,
sadistically dragging them past
seductive caloric bombshells,
do not pass go!

Between the chocolate Chips Ahoy (Ahoy matey!)
and those satanic Hostess cupcakes staring me down,
I think I may have a shot, unbeknownst to my distracted wife
an imminent grazer is what you've got!

Snickers Pie

2 sheets puff pastry
½ cup mascarpone
½ cup cream cheese
¼ cup caster sugar
3 eggs
2 cups Mars Snickers
6 servings

A sip-topian society

In the future, equitable circumstances will prevail
among chocolate malt drink holders, the banter
light and optimistic between sips
of sugar spiked Folgers.

The rights of all citizens to fulfill their
refreshment destiny inalienable, all will
submit to a higher sip-topian principle
of expresso order unassailable.

Generous chunks of caramel added piece and
24 count assorted donut security,
finally sprinkles will reign!!!
Washed down with splashes
of french vanilla surety.

Let hydration justice ring from Hollywood
to Taj Mahal, with latte abundance
and foodilicious beverages for all!!

Vanilla Latte

1 ¾ cups 2% milk
2 tablespoons vanilla flavored syrup
1 (1.5 fluid ounce) jigger brewed expresso
1 serving

The basil king

All bow before his quintessential herbal majesty,
a regal minted bearing signifying summer versatility.

Here comes his basil Excellency, gingerly riding
upon horse radish, its powerful cloves parsley kelp in
thyme with its horsetail hops, yet it brigham tea
wherever it willow and still makes soups,
sauces and sorbets pops.

The basil king dismounts into his kitchen kingdom
completely comfrey in his pennyroyal skullcapped,
waving his goldenseal scepter, eyebright, sage words
plantain themselves pesto enwrapped.

Thusly, he exercises his aromatic willow to enliven
pantry dishes ring, Cilantro! Tarragon to senna
out the spice rack word; "All hail the basil king!"

Basil pesto aioli condiment

4 tablespoons fresh basil, one large handful of leaves
1 tablespoon garlic, minced, about 2-3 cloves
½ cup vegetable oil
¼ cup virgin olive oil
½ teaspoon kosher salt
1 teaspoon lemon juice
2 egg yolks
8 servings

Flavor destinations

Tangy on the taste buds tango in Tasmania,
flavor destinations earned all fanned by foodie mania.

Tempting tummy tantalizers tenaciously Tibetian,
whimsically exotic dishes forecasted from
Timor to Turkmenistan.

Seasoned senses scintillated from
Senegal to Singapore, bombastic
belly buster boasting from
Bangladesh to Banglador.

Cubano International Sandwich

1 round flat focaccia bread
4 slices Boar's Head deli ham
4 slices Boar's Head deli chicken breast
4 slices swiss cheese
Add mild German mustard
Add chipotle mayonnaise
Add bread and butter pickle slices
Add garlic flavored butter for brushing on bread to grill
2-4 servings

Stop it! Stop it!

I'm sitting right here, I can see you,
silently casting your condemnatory
veggie aspersions! Stop it!!
So what it if I gag on bland,
squishy Brussels sprouts stewing in
dishwater....Mmmm! let me at them!!

Don't impale me if I also find
the soupy excuse for summer
squash equally vapid.
(canned and passed off as fresh)

Now that Porterhouse steak is
looking mighty fin...Ouch!
Hey, what did I just say about that?
Help! Meat police!! Arrest that
snobby vegan brat!!!

Grilled Steak and Potatoes with Garlic-herb butter

1 ½ lb. baby potatoes, halved
2 tablespoons olive oil
Salt and pepper
2 tablespoons unsalted butter, softened
1 tablespoon minced fresh parsley
5 garlic cloves, minced
1 ½ lb. sirloin steak, sliced into thin pieces
Add garlic-herb butter
4 servings

Chocolate cake falling

Mission control: chocolate mousse images picking up
chocolate cake falling, space shuttle moving to intercept course.
Super computer is calculating the two scoop vanilla
bean ice cream spin, factoring chocolate lover's
velocity with gravitational whipped cream trajectory
to ensure proper oral meshing of the
high lip smack coefficient.

Mission control: The cake has landed!
The cake has landed right in our mouths!
Thanks to the delicious efforts
of our crack caramel and
chocolate sauce teams...Oh no!
Another chocolate cake falling!
I repeat, another.....

Swedish chocolate cake

¼ cup plain flour
½ cup butter, melted
1 tablespoon vanilla extract
1 1/5 cup caster sugar
2 eggs
1 pinch of salt
2 tablespoons cocoa powder
6 servings

Thyme waits for no one

Please, I know you can parsley keep your bayleafs
to yourself, just stop whining about how there is not
enough thyme in your recipes to get things done,
I'm sorry that thyme leaves us short to get the
lemon roasted chicken properly prepared
so you can eat and run.

Must prioritize thyme for all foods important:

-Tea thyme
-Nectarine crumble thyme
-Butter maple biscuits thymed just right
-Vodka lemonade, always on thyme
-Definitely want to make thyme to rub down steaks
-No thyme for bacon? ...Now your life is simply unbalanced.

Vodka thyme lemonade

12 whole lemons
2 cups sugar
2 cups water
15 sprigs Fresh thyme, plus more for garnish
7 ounces Vodka
Add club soda
1 whole lemon cut into wedges for garnish
6 servings

Who says sorbet cantaloupe?

What a grape nation we live in, we can:

- drive each other bananas
- entertain a sense of wondering mints
- have the right to eat forbidden fruits
(despite creating many jams for ourselves and others)

So I don't know why sorbet cantaloupe?
It is high time to unlimit ourselves from just
orange or just blackberry sorbet, indeed,
we must dissolve our sweetened fears, pour
our imaginations into larger sorbet containers.
Process new melon and lime juice thoughts till smooth,
yes, taste it now, yes, why sorbet cantaloupe into my mouth?
I don't know why.

No-churn melon sorbet

1 tablespoon lemon juice

2 lb. cantaloupe or honeydew melon, diced and chilled

½ cup water

½ cup sugar

1 teaspoon lemon zest

1/3 cup light corn syrup

2 servings

Applied rib mathematics

In calculating heated rib factor optimization,
a mathematical barbecue isaucelian approach
can effectively be applied with high geometric
flavor probability to the grilling at hand.

This done in tandem with computational coleslaw,
baked bean physics and algebraic corn on the cobbinatorics.
Number theory can isolate the social choice of
fluid beer dynamics with random taste variables
ultimately reduced to the delicious.

Sweet mesquite barbeque ribs

2 tablespoons favorite dry rubs mesquite BBQ
2 pounds pork or beef spare ribs
1 cup favorite hickory smoke barbecue sauce
4 servings

Blueberry cobbler ambition

I've always wanted to be cobbler Big & Rich,
the center of dessert attention, "The"
desire of foodies that quells the hankering
and answers baking apprehension.

So big, my name tricked out in country fair lights,
so rich, people can't get enough of my big blueberried sights.

Hope someday to make my own family crest,
I will leave my mark, my destiny
with the horizontally blest.

Skillet blueberry cobbler

1 ½ pints fresh or thawed blueberries
½ teaspoon salt
1 ½ teaspoons baking powder
2 tablespoons unsalted butter
1 teaspoon cinnamon
¾ cup sugar
1 ¼ cups all purpose flour
2 teaspoons corn starch
2 tablespoons water
1 tablespoon lemon juice
¾ cup whole milk
1 teaspoon vanilla extract
5 tablespoons butter, cut into small cubes
8 servings

Nibbler on the loose

This is chief chocolate officer putting out an all
points bulletin to all M&M's:

"Be on the lookout for nibbler at large!
Suspect's mouth and hands are warmed
and extremely dangerous. Stay calm
and stay clear of all snack bowls and
vending machines. Only traverse
well lighted kitchens, pantries
and bulk snack aisles.

Do not, I repeat, do not snack it alone!
Perpetrator has a prodigious penchant for
anthropomorphic pretzel and peanut
spokespersons in plain attire. Don't melt
in his mouth or in his hands.
Forewarned is forearmed."

M&M's cookies

2 cups whole M&M's plain candies
1 cup packed brown sugar
¾ cup granulated sugar
1 teaspoon vanilla
2 eggs
2 ½ cups all-purpose flour
¾ teaspoon baking soda
¾ teaspoon salt
1 cup butter, softened
20 servings

Baconomics

Trending in today's top CNN stories:

-"Baconsoft will release its highly tasty 8bacon again platform that is hoped will fix the previous system bug of frying its pork servers when overdone."

-"The long awaited sequel of the fast and the furious bacon franchise: The taste of the furious: Master Chew! is now grilling in theaters this weekend."

-"Breakfast billionaire Warren Buffet is opening his 100th breakfast franchise promising investors that he will wow customers with triple! You heard right, triple bacon offerings!!"

-"Transbacon Airline's president has just fried up a statement only allowing a 2 pack of bacon limit per passenger carry on. This has created a firestorm of controversy with the Bacon is Meat Candy Coalition who decry unconstitutional bacon limiting flight policies."

Praline bacon

1 pound thick cut bacon
2 ½ ounces light brown sugar, about 6 tablespoons
1 ½ ounces pecan halves
1 serving
https://www.foodnetwork.com/recipes/alton-brown/praline-bacon-recipe-1949714

The Munchoreo Candidate

Shhh! A runaway snackspiracy
is fomenting in our midst. Oh, its
sickening how the cookie crumbles.

Ok, ok, I've got to stay focused, here it is, a puppet Oreo
candidate is running for Nabisco office that will only munch
on snacks dictated by corrupt milk and cookie interests!!!

This is so deliciously complicated in all its parts,
reaching the highest levels of our crunched bureaucracy...
(Rudely intrusive guard yelling 'Hey you in the cupboard')
Yikes! My foodie cover is blown, got to run! Foodies unite!!!

No-bake Oreo layer dessert

1 (15.35 ounce) package Double Stuff Oreo Cookies

½ cup butter, melted and slightly cooled

8 ounces cream cheese

1 cup powdered sugar

1 (8 ounce) tub Cool Whip

1 (5.1 ounce) box instant chocolate pudding

3 ½ cups milk

2 servings

A night of poultry

We will dress down chicken prime,
minced scallion, parsley, mint and lime.

Unabashed, we will face down the bulghur
and the tabouleh with coarsely chopped pecans,
orange salad, rosemary brewed, savory
chicken chopped, sliced, creamed,
chili fried and herb roasted stewed.

That famous fowl is quite the international sensation,
whether Jamaican, Oriental, or Mediterranean.

Adjust the bowtie pasta and get the cooking styled just right,
poultry is in the house and in the spotlight all night.

Chicken and cauliflower with herbed butter sauce

8 chicken thighs (about 7 oz. each)

¼ cup olive oil, divided

1 head cauliflower (about 2 lbs.) broken into small pieces

1 cup dry white wine

2 small shallots, fine chopped (about 3 tablespoons)

4 garlic cloves, finely chopped

3 tablespoons unsalted butter

2 tablespoons finely chopped parsley

4 servings

Are you horizontally blessed?

Gifted for caloric greatness?
Genius levels of stored energy potentials?
A bariatric Nobel Laureate?

Then you should only snack on foodie treats
commensurate with your wide dignified bearing,
creating even a new field called horizontal
food science engineering!
Blessed plumpdom triumphs!

Rich mud pie

16.5 ounces NESTLE TOLL HOUSE
Refrigerated chocolate chunk cookie bar dough
1 pint coffee ice cream, softened
8 ounces frozen whip topping, thawed
½ cup fudge sauce, warmed
2 tablespoons pecans, chopped, optional
1 crisp chocolate graham cracker crust
1 serving

When tempered mints flare

Different mints don't always work together,
short tempered little menthols to say the least.
I get stabbed mostly by spearmints,
persnickety about their fancied spot,
nearly strangled by intense peppermints who just
won't be smacked on like the rest of the minted lot.

Just cannot get used
to wintergreen's hostile
icy flavor crystal stare,
got to be careful this
aromatic genus
if bruised can be a bear.

Want scary? Mix them together and foment
taste bud sparks, incite fiery mouth/brain
rattling that induces tears,
don't say you were not warned
when tempered mints flare.

Andes mint cookies

1 Betty Crocker SuperMoist devil's food cake mix
1 whole egg
½ cup vegetable oil
½ cup Andes crème de menthe baking chips or
½ cup Andes crème de menthe mints
½ serving

One pack mind

Six pack that is, never felt so Miller lite and free,
having gone to the Coor of my bottled menagerie's.

IPA a lot for therapist to guiness me past this draught,
the Blue Moon swings and the Angry Orchards six pack
style is what I fought.

After a period of emotional lows I'm feeling Heineken,
my friends Samuel Adams and Stella are so happy to
see the Corona Extra in my step again.

I've sought and found new ways to make my life Budweiser,
and best of all I would like to introduce my new love,
Yuengling, a traditional lager sympathizer.

Michelada (Mexican beer cocktail)

4 tablespoons sea salt
6 lime
Add Mexican lager, corona
Add Worcestershire sauce or Tabasco sauce to serve
1 serving

Starry eyed snackers

I, I just loved snackaprio in that overindulgent movie
gut buster Tightanic! It was soo bloatmantic!!
His love interest and him gorged on Klondike
bars till the end...never let go! Never Let GO!!

Oh!.. I'm so deliriously hungry right now, no wait!
Could I be mixing this up with that Shakespearean food
tragedy where snackaprio is a pack of Oreo's and she has
a tall glass of milk and no regrets!?
Oh boy! I just need a snack.
Someone? Please?

Klondike Ice box cake

10 Original Klondike Bars
2 jars marshmallow fluff
2 ½ cups whipping cream
2 tablespoons vanilla
1 sleeve honey graham crackers
Add caramel syrup
Add chocolate syrup
Add chocolate hard shell
2 servings

Diving for sweetness

Time to Godiva for richness captured in caramel smoothness,
watch out for the Ghirardelli fish, one taste and your tooth
is now sweet all right through this.

In pursuit of cocoa powdered treasures,
one can go peanuts reaching into the recess
of confectioned pleasures.

At 20,000 naughtical treats one has entered
a dark chocolate world of flavonol eats, intensely
dark, Green and Blacks, Dark Blackout meets,
trust me Amano, this level of dark requires a real
Pascha for delightful, even organic Moseroth sweets.

Dark Chocolate truffles

1 cup favorite dark chocolate, broken into small pieces
¾ cup double whipping cream
Add cocoa powder, icing sugar or finely chopped nuts for
Rolling and dusting
¼ serving

Save room for dessertations

Be careful, ever so careful to run afoul of room for
delightful dessertations, the crème del a crème of
foodistic preparations.

The feast de resistance of culinary daliant consumption,
a veritable virtuoso of vainglorious presumption.

A curated bougie experience not to disappoint,
a fantastic foodtopia, so let's get the proverbial
fine dining "grub on" in this here joint.

Fine dining quail

4 quails, removed the leg from the joint and deboned the breast
6 clove garlic, finely chopped
1 ounce thyme oil
1 ounce rosemary oil
1 shallot, roughly chopped
1 teaspoon freshly ground black pepper
1 cup duck fat
Add black mustard micro greens
Add basil micro greens
Add radish shoots
2 servings

Just whip it

Cracked ice chips
Chocolate chips
Coconut milk
Peanut butter snack
When bananas come along, you must whip it!
When almonds hang around, you must whip!
Now when honey makes it strong, you must whip it!
Now whip it
Taste great
Mix it up
Drink it
Sip it
Chug it down
Make shakes
It's not too sweet
So whip it
Whip it good

Chocolate Almond Dream Smoothie

2 cups dark chocolate almond milk, ice cold
1 generous scoop Almond butter
2 tablespoons vanilla extract
2 large banana's, precut into small slices and frozen
2 servings

Jam lives!

Joie de vivre: for love of life! The blackberry
kind between the cracker and the crunch,
the strawberry kind for late night
snacks smothered till brunch.

Heartily live well as it pleases, varied jams consorted,
at that, among fruits and cheeses assorted.

A humble blueberry chap next to dignified lemon curd,
in an age of fast, preservative laden options, jam lives!
Or haven't you heard? For those bereft
of the social jam graces, a word...

Currant Jam

4 cups black currants
2 cups jam sugar
3 tablespoons raspberry brandy
2 limes, juiced and zested
24 servings

At the borderline of my plates

Is this the dinner destiny of caloric fates?
Doomed am I! Only to consume the dull and
mundane at the borders of all my plates?

How I pine away for the excitement of chicken fricassee,
the delight of foreign chef's expanding plated forte,
from Paris to Ha Long Bay.

Culinary dulling ought to be a crime,
Help! I'm trapped by my plate!
Masticated malfeasance I tell you! Well.....?
Don't just do something, stand their!

Desperate men and women on the plated edge
do ponder jumping...no...no... I can't.
Too constrained by fear, so ashamed of the obligatory.
Enlightened foodies save me from that which I hate ....
from the edge of my plate.

Chicken Fricassee with vermouth

1 ½ pounds ready to cook chicken, cut into serving pieces
Add salt, if desired
Add ground pepper
3 tablespoons butter
1 cup onions, finely chopped
4 cloves of garlic
2 tablespoons of flour
¾ cup dry white vermouth
¼ cup chicken broth
1 bay leaf
1 ounce thyme oil
1 cup heavy cream
4-6 servings

Beware the soldier of Doves

Ten-hut! Chocolatered regiments marching in step
to the dictates of dark cocoa pleadings,
munching smoothly through
the delectable hinterland
of tastebud leadings.

Unwrap! Unwrap! Hut1! Hut2! Too committed to
the cause, caught in the militarism of obligatory
confectionary deficiency.

Am I a volunteer soldier of velvet,
brown squared divinity?
Or drafted in recompense for
unbridled indulgence,
punished for delectable duplicity?

Save yourselves! It's too late for me!
(Forward! Marching with chocolate eating efficiency)

Espresso-Dove Chocolate cookies

24 dark chocolate Dove squares

1 cup light brown sugar

½ cup granulated sugar

1 tablespoon vanilla extract

2 tablespoons instant expresso

1 teaspoon Medaglia D'oro, if desired

2 tablespoons heavy cream

1 egg

¼ teaspoon baking soda

2 ¼ cups all-purpose flour

4 servings

Constitutionally fried chicken

Our nation has a rich, savory history:

Who was the 1st freed deep fried black meat chicken?
Crispus Maximus

Who was nation's best leading chicken during the Civil war?
Abraham Lickin

A former chicken slave turned delicious?
George Washington Carved up

Who was one of the 1st chicken signers of constitution who
died before completing 2nd term in House fryer?
Abraham Butterballdwin

Which confederate chicken general got himself in a lot of hot
water?
Alexander Campbell chicken soups

Chicken fried chicken

5 boneless skinless chicken breasts
(Butterflied and pounded ¼ inch thick)
2 cups all purpose flour, dredging
1 tablespoon chicken seasoning
4 eggs beaten
2 cups chicken stock
½ cup milk
1 ounce thyme oil
Add salt and pepper
2 servings

Regular broccoli massage is important

If one must stalk their broccoli, get steamed for its
percent of daily value, thine flowering crest,
or sautee this super food in oil and butter,
a touch of salt for added zest.

Slowly, cooking it down from its green crown,
modestly while on its trunk tread lightly
upon edible renown.

Briskly I will rub thee with cheese vigor,
letting the imagination sprout,
so much more quickly I will
spearhead your devouring,
savoring each massaged morsel
without a doubt.

RITZ broccoli Casserole

36 RITZ Crackers, coarsely crushed, about 1 ½ cups, divided
¾ pound VELVEETA, cut into ½ inch cubes
3 packages (10 ounces each) broccoli, frozen chopped, thawed, drained
¼ margarine or butter, melted
8 servings
http://www.kraftrecipes.com/recipes/ritz-broccoli-casserole-56398.aspx?kraftcustom=true

Vengeful juicing

Do you hate them?
(fruits and veggies of course)
Do you desire to see blood?
The blood of pressed contempt for fruit,
sieving with envy, fiber dances,
through plastic and metal
housing electric motor romances.

The more feeding, the more chopping,
the more apples are made grater,
the fibrous blood expressed
is bad turned goodness
for the carrot eating hater.

Centrifugal forces spun separate fruit and vegetable matter,
antioxidant dense rage unleashed in the accelerated splatter.

Hey, take out your frustrations on juiced foods not people.

Sunrise citrus juice

2 apples
2 grapefruits, peeled
1 red bell pepper, capsicum
2 pears
8 carrots
Juicer required
2 servings

Carrot cake fated

What is your future likened to?
Will it be filled with grated raw carrot moments,
chopped in delightful walnut measures?
Time taken to appreciate sugar sweetened
moments and crushed pineapple pleasures?

Balanced cinnamon and spice tastefully recruited,
oiled eggstravagantly. I know, you think my speech
is floury, no two words salted the same,
all that matters is how you combine the
ingredients of a good life for baked fame,
to not pause in the cool cream cheese frosted
finish would be the greatest shame.

3 layer Carrot Cake

2 ½ cups all-purpose flour, plus more for pans
1 teaspoon baking soda
¾ teaspoon coarse salt
¼ teaspoon ground nutmeg
1 cup packed light-brown sugar
3 large eggs
½ cup water
2 cups pecans (1 cup finely chopped for batter,
1 cup coarsely chopped for decorating sides of cake)
1 teaspoon baking powder
1 teaspoon ground cinnamon
½ teaspoon ground ginger
 3 sticks (12 ounces) unsalted butter, room temperature
Plus more for pans
½ cup granulated sugar
2 teaspoons pure vanilla extract
1 pound carrots (8 to 10 medium carrots), peeled and shredded
On a box grater or in a food processor (about 2 ¾ cups)
Easy cream cheese frosting for carrot cake
4 servings
https://www.marthastewart.com/356827/carrot-cake

Miss Piggy's rap album

Playlist:

Kung Pao chicken girl
Food gangsta's plight
.38 in store lunch specials
Stone cold waffles
Cereal killa
Premeditated marbling
Put a little cheese in it
Big Shrimpin
Quit hatin on by bacon!
Hotwings gettin jiggy
Brownies all up in my snout
Bout to get phat wings
Slap it on a bun baby....with some sauerkraut... don't forget the
ketchup...
You know how I spice it
Finger on my loaded baked potato

Miss Piggy Cocktail

2 Southern Comfort
4 WKD Red
2 Port
1 serving
https://makemeacocktail.com/cocktail/3446/miss-piggy/
https://www.goodreads.com/book/show/485461.In_the_Kitc
hen_with_Miss_Piggy

Whirled peas possible

All we have to do is start from scratch,
beet our peas-like inclinations and if you
have to make a fresh batch.

Be careful what you cauliflower, no chive talkin allowed,
now is as good a thyme as any to ponder at ease,
what cayenne I do to promote more whirled peas?

Like not fishing for
solutions and then getting
orange roughy with each other,
let's instead move gingerly to a warmer
whirled encompassing dilution between my
 deep stir and your butter.

Truly, we must cool it down and sea past our salt differences
and the best pearled onions in interacting transparencies,
now take off the cover of a pot brimming with whirled
possibilities.

Split Pea Soup

1 pound split peas, rinsed
2 pounds bone-in ham piece, ham shank or other
1 ounce thyme oil
2 .5 quarts water
2 onions, minced
2 celery ribs, chopped
3 small new potatoes, scrubbed and chopped
Salt and pepper, to taste
2 tablespoons fresh lemon juice, optional
2 medium garlic cloves, minced
1 tablespoon extra virgin olive oil, optional
8 servings

Candy works

Don't think for a moment concentrated sweets
can't get it done, they work their tootsie rolls off,
for peanuts at that but no worries
the victory will soon be won.

They won't stop until they reach the reese's
of their potential, just take it to the Milky Way,
all else is inconsequential.

Crazy Payday's are coming,
going from Zero to $100
Grand in each hand, wait
until Reggie and Clark find out how
Chunky Baby Ruth got running a
Marathon candy plan.

Finally, Hershey is so successful, despite the Gogo clusters
and the Rocky Roads, now everyone is rollin phat, if you
think all you can gain from candy is empty calories
then Charleston Chew on that.

Candy bar pie

2 cups candy bars, chopped and extra candy for the top
¾ cup plain flour
½ teaspoon of salt
½ cup butter
2 tablespoons or more of ice water
1 cup brown sugar
¼ cup unsalted butter, softened
1 large egg
2 teaspoons vanilla extract
1 teaspoon baking powder
3 servings

Oh boy, he's Heineken

Every time we meet the big green guy at the pub
must we go thru this bragging about the beer stats throttle?
I know, I know, you're the famous Dutch lager with the
lone star on the green bottle.

No surprise that you're a huge multinational beer brand,
the domestically brewed champion hails from Amsterdam.

Did you know...Yes! You've got heaps of money and you
look great for your brewing age! Can we go now?
You know, change things up now and then,..No!
I don't want to hear about all the beer brands you
own..Oh boy, he's really Heineken.

Heineken barbeque chicken

1 12oz. bottle Heineken beer
1/3 cup favorite honey barbecue sauce
2 tablespoons black pepper
½ chicken, bird
4 cloves garlic, minced
Side dish potatoes
2-3 servings

Banana ooh nana!

Ooh banana ooh nana! I had banana ensalada ooh nana.
I sliced and placed it ensalada ooh nana.

O, O, O, O!
I had the bacon and brie with the salad fonte.
O, girl!!
I got nana's for you, nana's for me.
Baby O!
I'll order two more with a 2nd entrée.

Ooh banana ooh nana
Banana ensalada ooh nana

Ooh banana's from Havana, sweet, sautéed, fried platana.
Banana ooh nana!

Tropical fruit smoothie

2-3 medium frozen and thinly sliced bananas
2-3 cups of fresh finely chopped pineapples
2 cups fresh squeezed orange juice
1-2 cups ice optional
2 servings

Black forest cake downed!

Mayday! Mayday!
Black forest cake downed!!
I repeat, black forest cake downed!!

Cake Boss requesting immediate backup!
Alpha-Charley-Taco
Surprise party insurgents attacking from all sides,
these senior citizens are relentless...
Hurry! Even the crumbs
are being overwhelmed.

Look out! Eleven o'clock,
knives and forks coming in hot!!
Mayday! Mayday......

Black forest cake

10 cherries
1 cup all purpose flour
1 cup freshly whipped cream
1 ½ cups sweetened condense milk
3 tablespoons cocoa powder
1 teaspoon baking powder
1 teaspoon cooking soda
½ cup butter
1 cup aerated cola drink
1 pinch of salt
½ cup dairy milk chocolate
6-8 servings

Eminem foodie chant

A two for one special I know it don't matter,
but I was so hungry I smoked the whole platter.

And as I continue this story gets sadder,
light up the lunch menu keep taxing my bladder.

Subdue my mad chewing so others won't scatter.
I went from fast foodie to plate to plate swagger,
How can I stop choking down cookie dough batter???

It's the foodie, the munching, the crunching
On rye, wheat or sourdough, (yo!)
Drink specials are one shots, combined with the garlic knots
Their so terrific you just can't let it go (you better..)
(Repeat)

Garlic Knots

1 ounce garlic oil

1 can Pilsbury Golden Layers Buttermilk Biscuits

1 teaspoon dried oregano

1 teaspoon dried parsley flakes

3 tablespoons parmesan cheese, grated

¼ cup canola oil

8 servings

Alcohol intimacy

You know how tasteful life can be after 5pm,
2 for 1 specials all good as we saunter to ballads of Kem.

Really, I want to make mimosa of the time I spend with you,
a Bailey's Irish Cream come true.

Each moment an extra
Chardonnairy experience,
unsteady as it goes, every
relationship has its black label
high's and its occasional merlot's.

How ironic, meeting as we did like gin and tonic.

All too soon mixed drinks move too fast and make
things crazy like a fox, with all alcohol
intimacies ending like Jameson or
Jack Daniels....on the rocks.

Long Island Iced Tea

Captain Morgan Original Spiced Gold
Smirnoff No. 21 Vodka
Gordon's London Dry Gin
Orange liquer
Don Julio Blanco Tequila
Sugar syrup
Lemon juice
Lime juice
Fill a cocktail shaker with ice cubes and equal amounts of each
spirit
Cola
1 slice lemon as garnish
1 serving
https://uk.thebar.com/recipe/long-island-iced-tea

Can it already

Save the good fruitage of your labors,
then there will be plenty to share with
all of your neighbors.

No forbidden fruitage, let us not forget
the kind that create many jams,
like the supersized tubs
discounted deeply at Sams.

Everyone must exercise due diligence, earnest effort,
the sweat of hard work ethic, can immediately
ferment hot to sweetly kinetic.

Get used to working feverishly despite under seasonal pressure,
savoring this preserve is already my pleasure.

Homemade strawberry jam

6 (12 ounce) jars with lids
6 pounds of fresh strawberries
3 cups granulated sugar
6-12 servings

The Chronicles of a Shakemaster

Episodes:
The total shake down
Beware the seven zesty lemons
Shake down protocol #20
Shake baby shake, make one take out please
High ya! Frappe a latte
Shake the temptations
Focusology of the shake mind
Shake craftiness
Find the inner dreamsicle
Don't knock it till you shake it

Orange dreamsicle shake

2 large bananas, thinly sliced and frozen
¼ container orange juice concentrate
2 tablespoons sweetened condense milk
3 tablespoons vanilla extract
1 cup orange soda
1 serving

About the Author:

A Tampa bay area poet who has seen an excellent culinary cultural transformation in artful dining experiences that continues to attract the attentions of foodies everywhere. He has been married to wife Victoria for 15 years, who considers herself to be an unabashed foodie as well. Who knows, we just may see you at the corner of ambiance and great food.

Other book titles also by author for purchase thru Ingram Sparks, Amazon and other fine retailers:

Dances in the theater of the mind

Nurses bred for Business:
The Awakening of Legions of Nurse Entrepreneurs

Rhythmic Elegance:
A poetic treatise on our place in the universe

Acknowledgments

This section is an attempt by the author to thank every possible source of inspiration and every backer for this nutty and whimsical creative work:

ProKitchen: shared kitchen & culinary incubator
Food Network shows:
Chopped
Iron Chef America
The Kitchen
Diners, Drive-Ins and Dives
Worst Cooks in America
Barefoot Contessa
The Great Food Truck Race
Ace of Cakes
Unwrapped
Rachel vs. Guy: Celebrity Cook-Off
TLC's Cake Boss
All Hollywood Celebrities
ABC's The Chew
Oprah Winfrey Network
The Rachael Ray Show
Dr Oz
Dr Phil

Steve Harvey
Harry
CBS
NBC
CNN
ESPN
Tyler Perry Studios
Christopher Steinocher, President and CEO of the St.
Petersburg area Chamber of Commerce
St. Petersburg Mayor Rick Kriseman
Former St. Pete Mayor Rick Baker
Nestle
PepsiCo
The Coca-Cola Company
JBS
Kerry Group
Campbell Soup Company
Yili Group
Parmalat
Daniels Midland Company
Anheuser-Busch InBev
Mondelez International
SABMiller
Tyson Foods
Cargill
Mars
Unilever

Danone
Heineken
Lactalis
Kirin Holdings
Asahi Group
Suntory
Kraft Foods Group
Diageo
General Mills Inc.
DMK Deutsches Milchkonter
Ajinomoto
The Hershey Company
Oetker Group
Red Bull
Sodiaal
China Mengniu
Dairy Company
McCain Food Limited
Morinaga Milk Industry
Muller Group
Grupo Modelo (Mexico)
Ingredion Inc.
Nissui
Bongrain
Dr Pepper Snapple Group
LVMH
McCormick Corporation
The J.M. Smucker Company

Royal FrieslandCampina

Fonterra

ConAgra Foods Inc.

Brf Brasil Foods

CHS Inc.

Kellog Company

Arla Foods

Grupo Bimbo (Mexico)

Smithfield Foods

NH Foods

Associated British Foods

Pernod Ricard

Femsa

Carlsberg

Meiji Holdings

HJ Heinz Company

Ferrero

Bacardi

Nisshin Seifun Group

Itoham Foods

Sapporo Holdings

Tate & Lyle

Ito En

Barilla

ThaiBev

Maxingvest/Tchibo

Nissin Foods Group

Barry Callebaut
Coca-Cola Amatil
Schreiber Foods
Land O' Lakes Inc
Coca-Cola West
QP Corporation
Bunge
Vion
Sudzucker
Danish Crown
Yamazaki Baking
Coca-cola HBC
Maruha Nichiro Corporation
Marfrig Group
Saputo
Dean Foods Company
Hormel Foods Corporation
Coca-Cola Enterprises
Tsingtao Brewery
Maple Leaf Foods
Dole Food Company, Inc
Molson Coors Brewing Company
JR Simplot
Japan Tobacco International
Hilshire Brands
Del Monte Foods Company
Groupe Bel
Agropur Cooperative

DE Master Blenders 1753
E. & J. Gallo Winery
Contemporary Periodontics & Implant Dentistry
St. Anthony's Foundation
Heartbeat international Foundation(HBI)
America's Test Kitchen
The Culinary Institute of America
Phoenix3 marketing

Great restaurants in Tampa Bay area:

Sea Salt
Rococo Steak
Birch & Vine
Marchand's Bar and Grill
Trip's Diner
Leverock's Great Seafood
Parkshore Grill
400 Beach Seafood and Tap House
Mazzaro's Italian Market
Jack's London Grill
The Canopy Rooftop Lounge
BellaBrava
Bodega Comida Cantina Café
Trip's Diner
Casita Taqueria
Skyway Jack Restaurant

Gratzzi Italian Grille
The Mill
Noble Crust
Cassis American Brasserie
The Hanger Restaurant & Flight Lounge
Munch's Sundries & Restaurant
Kissin' Cuzzins Neighborhood
Tap Room
Moon Under Water
Hawkers Asian Street Fare
Red Mesa
Engine No. 9
Texas Roadhouse
Annata Wine Bar
Cody's Original Roadhouse
Chiefs Creole Café
Harold Seltzer's Steakhouse
URBAN Brew and BBQ
Fourth Street Shrimp Store
Stillwaters Tavern
Brick & Mortar
Café Gala
La V
Harvey's 4th Street Grill
Mid Peninsula Seafood
Red Mesa Mercado
Dead Bob's
Pipo's Original Cuban Café

Beau & Mo's Italian Eating House
The Oyster Bar
The Getaway
The Cider Press Café
Ll Ritorno
Pom Pom's Tea House & Sandwicheria
PoFolks
Fresco's Waterfront Bistro
Courtside Grille
Hofbrauhaus St. Petersburg
The Burg Bar and Grill
Pizza Box
Metro Diner
The Avenue
Toby's Original Little Italy Pizza
El Cap
Reading room Restaurant
Leafy Green Café
Rae Rae's Café
Ruth Chris Steak House
9 Bangkok Restaurant
Nitally's
Urban Comfort
Ciccio Cali
TiKanis
The Lemon Grass
Bonefish Grill

Three Birds Tavern

Love Food Central

Nueva Cantina

Alesia

Acropolis Greek Taverna

Madfish

Chattaway

Tryst

St. Pete Brewing Company

Ferg's Sports Bar & Grill

The Melting Pot

The Bubba Gump Shrimp Co. Restaurant and Bar

Carmelita's Mexican Restaurant

Green Bench Brewing Company

Texas Cattle Company

Kristina's Café

Café Cibo

O' Bistro

Wooden Rooster

Rib City Restaurant

Gateway to India

Bavaro's Pizza Napoletana and Pastaria

The Pesky Pelican Brew Pub

Five Bucks Drinkery

Gianni's NY Pizza

Cracker Barrel

Dickey's Barbecue Pit

Tom+Chee

Paisano's Pizza N Pasta
Athenian Garden
Old Northeast Tavern
Cappy's Pizzeria
Fresh Kitchen
LUNA Restaurant & Lounge
Burger Monger
Parkside Café
Primos
Bern's Steakhouse
Maggiano's Little Italy
Columbia Restaurant
La Teresita Café
Ceviche Tapas Bar & Restaurant
Pino's Café
China Latina
Tapas Spanish Café
Todo Rico
Gold Ring Café & Catering
Copa's Latin America Café
La Bamba Spanish Restaurant
Taco Bus
Eddie & Sam's NY Pizza
Jackson's Bistro, Bar & Sushi
Bahama Breeze
Yummy House China Bistro
Big Apple Buffet

Tasty Pho
Urban Restaurant Group

Poetry sources I would like to acknowledge:

Oprah's Book Club
Poetry (Magazine)
Poetryfoundation.org
Poetrysoup.com
Academy of American Poets
The Poetry Society of America
Poets & Writers, Inc
Duotrope
New Pages
The Marin Poetry Center
Poets House
The Science Fiction Poetry Association
PennSound
Dallas Poets Community
The Concord Poetry Center
Haiku Society of America
The Poetry Center of Chicago
Star*Line
National Federation of State Poetry Societies
Poetry Journals
Poetry Flash
Arsenic Lobster Poetry Journal

Smartish Pace

Ploughshares

Poet Lore

Poetry Superhighway

Nostrovia Poetry

Cordite Poetry Review

Tule Review

Up the Staircase Quarterly

Slipstream Magazine

Aberration Labyrinth

Plume

Parody

Now Culture

Aberration Labyrinth

The Hollins Critic

Iodine Poetry Journal

Lexicon Polaroid

Abramelin

The Rotary Dial

Chaparral

Blast Furnace

The Araya Review

U.S.1 Poets' Cooperative

Visions-International

Boxcar Poetry Review

My Favorite Bullet

The Innisfree Poetry Journal

Leveler

The Cape Rock

Rattle

32 Poems

491 Magazine

Antiphon Poetry Magazine

Free Verse: A Journal of Contemporary Poetry & Poetics

Exercise Bowler

Acorn: a Journal of Contemporary Haiku

The Michigan Poet

Toad the Journal

Found Poetry Review

Watermark: A Poet's Notebook

The Poetry Archive

Fishouse

Poetry Quarterly

Poetry Northwest

American Poetry Review

Library of Congress Poet Laureate

All Poetry Blogs

Verse Daily

The Page

The Columbia Granger's World of Poetry

Electronic Poetry Center

Poetry Daily

Button Poetry

Apples and Snakes

Kalamazoo Poetry Festival

Urbana Poetry Slam
Nuyorican Poets Café
Write Out Loud
Geraldine R. Dodge Poetry Program
Chicago Slam Works
The Performance Poetry Preservation Project
Winning Writers
Book That Poet
For Better for Verse
The Writer's Almanac with Garrison Keillor
American Life In Poetry
Wave Books Erasures Tool
Contemporary American Voices